THE POWER OF A POSITIVE PERSPECTIVE

THE POWER OF A POSITIVE PERSPECTIVE

How challenging the lies you believe can help you live
the life God has planned for you.

FREMON WILLIAMS

THE PAPER HOUSE
PUBLISHING

Contents

I would like to dedicate this book to my wife, Darnelle, you have been nothing but supportive while writing this book and being my biggest cheerleader. To my children, you have taught me so much and helped me understand what matters most in life. To my pastor, thank you for shepherding, leading, challenging, and inspiring me so well. To our Church, you are a joy to be a part of. To my friends and family who read this, I pray it is a blessing to you!

ONE

The Lies We Believe

Did he *really* say that? Perhaps your life has been built on a foundation that is not 100% true. I want to live a life of full truth, not most, half, or a quarter of the truth. I don't want to get to the end of my life and realize what I was doing wasn't truly everything I was supposed to do. I want to be sure I am working from motivation that is 100% accurate. Maybe you want the same for your life; you want to be sure the things you believe provide a firm foundation.

Genesis 3:1-4 NIV

1 Now the serpent was more crafty than any of the wild animals the Lord God had made. He said to the woman, "Did God really say, 'You must not eat from any tree in the garden'?"

2 The woman said to the serpent, "We may eat fruit from the trees in the garden, 3 but God did say, 'You must not eat fruit from the tree that is in the middle of the garden, and you must not touch it, or you will die.'"

4 "You will not certainly die," the serpent said to the woman. 5 "For God knows that when you eat from it your eyes will be opened, and you will be like God, knowing good and evil."

In the beginning, Eve and Adam's core belief was tempted by one small adjustment of the truth, a change destined to alter all of humanity. It brought about sin that ultimately required Jesus' sacrificial death. I wonder what small lies we believe? Have we allowed seemingly insignificant lies to adjust our lives in a *big* way? What lies represent the foundation of our lives?

A good lie sounds like the truth. Little wonder Eve believed the serpent. Who wouldn't? The serpent was pretty clever. The serpent was filled with the devil who is the father of lies (John 8:44). He lied a lot and his words sounded pretty true. The serpent deceived our great ancestors is the same way he deceives us today. We fall prey to the lies because they sound like the truth. But it is our responsibility to do something about the lies we believe. I hope this book will help you stop and think about some of the lies you've believed. I want to replace them with the truth.

There were a lot of reasons for me to not write this book. I don't know enough. I don't have enough time. No one really knows me. I didn't know where to start. What if I can't get a publisher? I don't know how publishing works (as I am writing this chapter, I *still* don't know how it works). All these thoughts (lies) crept into my head. Allowing those lies to take precedence would kept me from beginning, let alone finishing this book. But I persevered. I kept pushing myself. I kept pursuing my purpose despite the lies assailing me every day. And while some of the reasons I shouldn't have started were accurate (not knowing how publishing works), it was the lie of "I can't write a book *because* I don't know about publishing" that I choose not to believe. There are plenty of legitimate circumstances in your life you cannot change. You have no control over where you were born, the family into which you were born, your past, your mistakes, your intellectual capabilities, and a host of other circumstance. But the question is: Do you believe these circumstances are roadblocks? That is a lie designed to keep you from moving forward. The facts cannot be changed, but "these things can hold me back" isn't real. In the words of Stephen Hawking, "However bad life may seem, there is always something you can do, and succeed at. While there's life, there is hope."[1]

It is crazy how we can allow one small lie to make a big difference in our lives. But you're not alone. Many people have been kept from making a difference. Why? Because they believed the lie. But the good news is there are many other people who choose to reject the small lie and made a big difference. Will you be someone who is held back by the lie or will you reject the lie and move forward in truth?

Your success in life is not predicated by how many lies you've been told (or not). It's determined by your ability to reject the lies. We've all believed lies, but it's the ones who reject those lies that continue to run on the track of life. Success is not the absence of lies; success is the ability to move forward in spite of the lies you face. In fact, the people who have faced the most opposition in life prove to be some of the most successful. Consider some of the patriarchs of the Christian faith. Moses had a speech problem; Peter was emotionally unstable; David had issues with women. Paul was previously a Christian killer. Every one of those reasons were opportunities for them to believe the lie of "God can't use me." But because they rejected the lie, they are now examples of success and encouragement. How many lives could you change if you reject the lies that have been keeping you from moving forward in truth?

There's a story of an 70 year old man who worked at a mail delivery warehouse. He sorted large boxes for delivery and loaded them into trucks. He did manual labor work day in and day out for many years. He was one of the hardest working men at the warehouse. He'd had a limp since he was 40 – nothing drastic, but noticeable. It hurt on occasion, but the old man never allowed the hurt to keep him from working hard. He was raised to believed that pain was a weakness. He kept at it so he could provide. The man had worked at the warehouse for 29 years and was on his last year before retirement. As retirement approached, the man worked harder. One day, his limp got worse. He tried to rebound from the pain and keep moving, but despite everything he did, the pain persisted. Still, he pushed past it.

He had a goal, a dream he had almost completed. With only weeks left until retirement, as he was walking with a box from one truck to another, he collapsed. The loud thud on the back of the metal truck loading dock could be heard around warehouse. His co-workers rushed to his aid. Seeing him in agony they picked him up and took him into the office. He couldn't walk. He pointed at his hip and said the pain was unbearable. They rushed him to the ER for an X-ray. The doctor walked out with a shocked look on his face.

"Sir, I am sorry to say, but you have a broken hip. But that's not the most interesting part. Based on the X-ray, your hip has been broken for years. It has healed incorrectly. The cartilage that developed over time to keep your hip in place has disintegrated and is the cause of your pain."

"How long before I can get back to work?" the man asked.

The doctor said, "In order for your hip to heal properly, we will need to re-break your hip and allow it to heal the correct way. With surgery and physical therapy, we expect you to be wheelchair bound for the next year and walking with a cane for the rest of your life."

The old man looked like he had seen a ghost; he couldn't believe what he was hearing. In an effort to maximize his take home pay and reduce his bills, he had not taken disability insurance or employed any other measure to provide income while he didn't work. No work – no pay. He had to continue working if he ever hoped to retire. All of the years of hard work would go down the drain.

Similar to the old man, many of us live with a "hip" problem (a wrong mindset or broken perspective) for so long that we accept it as truth. We go about our lives like there's nothing wrong when in reality, there is a limp, a lie that has so consumed our way of thinking we've stopped challenging it. Instead of us moving forward in our God given purposes, we sell ourselves short because of a lie we've believed for so long. God doesn't want you to keep from achieving all that He has for you because of a lie you've believed. Is a lie that you are currently believing, something preventing you from moving forward? What perspective clings to like a leech? ach? What would your life look like if you challenged the lie?

Do you remember when you realized Santa Claus wasn't real? Or when you found out that the Tooth Fairy was really your parents? There's a sense of shock whenever you find out the facts of a situation, event, thing, or person. But there is also relief. For example, what emotions come to you when you consider some of these facts? The letter "W" isn't actually double "U" its two "Vs" even though we pronounce it "double u." We call a particular fruit a "blue" berry even though it is acutely purple.

No emotion yet? Let's take it up a notch. Adam and Eve never ate an "apple." They consumed a "fruit." What about this one. In the last year of Dr. Martin Luther King, Jr.'s life, he was one of the most hated men in America. Do you believe that? A Harris Poll taken during King's last year showed that nearly three-quarters of the American people thought he was unacceptable or unwelcome, and almost 60% of his own people, Black Americans, thought he was irrelevant.[2]

These are facts and they are also perspective shifts. If we believe things only from one perspective, we can continue to believe a lie. Ninety-nine percent of the truth is still 100% of a lie. To achieve everything possible, we need to know the truth about everything.

Consider the Dr. King reference. He was not universally revered. His opposition did not come exclusively from racists. In fact, if we were opposed by the very people we were trying to help, many of us would be tempted to throw in the towel and quit.

I hope you want to achieve everything that God wants you to accomplish. Along the way, you're going to face wrong perspectives and lies you will need to challenge. Over the course of this book, we are going to look at the common lies we believe and challenge them with truth. I invite you to come on this journey to be all and to believe all that God wants.

Questions:

- What lie have you believed about yourself or your situations?
- What will your life look like if you choose to believe the truth about your situation?
- What do you believe God would say about you or your situation?

TWO

I Can't Do It

Have you ever told yourself, "There's no way I can do that?" It's something we say when we face an apparently impossible challenge. But have you ever asked yourself, "Why do I think I can't do it?"

Why are we so quick to doubt what we think we can do? It's not our fault. Think about how many times we heard the word "no" growing up. From the questions we asked like, "Can I have candy for dinner?" "No!" "Can I jump in the deep end?" "No!" "Can I watch TV all night?" "No!" What about the statements we were told: no running, no jumping, no hitting, no throwing, no − you fill in the blank. You get the picture. If you grew up like that, it's safe to say you've probably heard the word "no" far more than you heard the word "yes." Think about what hearing "the negative" does to a young boy or girl and how that translates to our teenage, young adult, and adult years. It can have an effect on our core beliefs about what we can and cannot accomplish. Perhaps we have been hardwired to have a perspective that first thinks of what we cannot do versus what we can do. That's the perspective I want to challenge in this chapter.

When our daughter was two months old, my wife and I purchased a shave ice business. It fell into our laps. We weren't looking to buy a business or to take on any additional responsibilities. I am in full-time ministry; my wife works full time. And we had just added a baby. There was no way we should have taken on something else. But my wife insisted we should "Look into it." Being a good husband, I did.

Things seemed more appealing than I thought or hoped they would. We prayed about it. "God if you want us to have this business, you're going to have to make this super easy for us and open up all the doors." And He did. The money and resources for the business came out of nowhere. We bought the business. We pulled money from some other investments, traded in an old car for a truck to pull the trailer, and managed to find employees. It was crazy how things fell into place even up to the opening day.

We needed an employee, so we started accepting applications and doing interviews. One by one, we went through applications and interviews. Things weren't looking too promising. After two weeks of trying to find someone to work, we were at a dead end and couldn't figure out what to do. It was a Sunday and we needed someone to work the next day. My wife and I woke up, got ready for church, and we said to ourselves, "God is going to have to work this one out." We didn't think twice about it.

While we were at church, a bright eyed, bubbly, sweet young woman walked up to me and asked, "Do you know of anyone who is hiring?" I chuckled and said. "Yes." She said, "Well great, because I really need a job. I just quit the one I had because my boss was rude and I need a job right away." I asked, "How soon can you start?" "Tomorrow" he said. I replied, "Well the job I am thinking of is our business, shave ice, but we would need to train you first."

She said, "Great, I am not doing anything after church." I laughed and said "No, you don't understand. We have to train you on how to operate the entire thing, make all the flavors, shave the ice and pour the syrup." She said, "I am a quick learner."

We trained her on Sunday night. She opened up the store the next day! Not only was she a quick learner, she was also one of our top performing employees. She received rave reviews about her exceptional customer service. We went from thinking "There's no way we can do this" to understanding the power of challenging the lie and trusting God.

You would think we would understand the principal after what happened, right? Nope! One day I was talking to a buddy of mine and he asked me how business was going. I said things were good, but with all the effort we had exerted,

I wasn't sure about the return. My exact words were, "It's not like we can make a million dollars running a shave ice businesses." He looked at me and said, "Yes you can. Matter of fact, someone else already has. If you don't believe me, Google it." I googled "$1 million shave ice business" and sure enough, several of them popped up. I was shocked and humbled. It made me question what other things might be possible? Is the phrase "I can't do it" a lie that I have believed? I wonder what things in your life you can achieve if you didn't believe the lie.

One of the biggest lies I hear people say is "I can't do it." Have you ever gotten to a place where you quit, gave up, or said it? Whether it's a workout, trying to forgive someone, starting something new, deciding to wake up early, or starting a new career, we're all going to face an obstacle or obstacles trying to convince us that we can't do it. You must make the decision to push past the lie.

One of my favorite scriptures is Philippians 4:13 (NKJV): "I can do all things through Christ who strengthens me."

This is also one of the most challenging verses because the question I have to ask myself is, "Do I really believe it?" There is nothing left out of "all." There is not one thing you cannot accomplish. But here is the kicker: "through Christ who strengthens me." You see, all things truly are possible when Christ is the one who gives you the strength to do it. With God, all things are possible (Matt. 19:26). When we attempt to do things in our own power and our own strength, it will only get us so far. At some point we will need to surrender our strength to the One who is mightier, stronger, and knows more than we do. I heard a pastor say something one day. It blew my mind. He said: "It's not about working harder, but surrendering more."

Think about how many plans we have or have had that we are completely reliant on ourselves to accomplish. How many of those plans succeed? I am pretty confident that the plans you have (or had) where God was not at the center either failed or soon will. I am not trying to be pessimistic or negative – just the opposite. Plans for your life will succeed. Plans for your life will prosper. You can do it. The question is: Whose plans are you following? God has plans for your life! And they are not just any type of plans; they are plans to prosper you, plans to give you hope and not harm you (Jeremiah 29:11). All God wants us to do is surrender our plans to His.

Even God's plans are not easy, but trusting God with His plans for our life builds our faith. And when our faith is built, we are stronger. Matthew 11:30 reads, "My yoke is easy and my *burden is light."* Does that mean life is easy? No, in fact there will still be burdens and problems, but if we come to Jesus with our life and our plans, He gives us the peace, joy, and strength in the midst of them. Ask yourself: "Do the plans for my life seem too heavy and too burdensome?" If so, they are probably plans that don't involve Jesus.

It will still be challenging to walk out the plans of God for your life. But understanding that they are God's plans and not yours will take a little pressure off. There have been plenty of instances in our marriage when things don't go as planned. We're late for something; we miss paying a bill; my wife gets into an accident. Somehow these are my fault. (If you're a married man, you can probably relate.)

But there is good news. Just as I take responsibility when things don't go right, we can give God the responsibility for the plans He has for our lives. And when we do, God takes our lives and builds something amazing.

There are so many great plans inside of you that God wants you to accomplish. He has good plans. They are exceedingly above all we can think, ask for or imagine (Ephesians 3:20).Unfortunately most of the time, the enemy knows what some of those plans more than we do. He tries to get us to believe the lie of, "I can't do it" – all to keep us from doing them. The enemy isn't fighting us fist to fist and toe to toe like we may think. The devil is clever; he's not powerful. So his fight is through craftiness. His fight is through deception and F.E.A.R. (False Evidence Appearing to be Real). The enemy uses small lies, small false statements like, "I can't do it" to cause us to make big choices, big decisions that affect the kingdom of God.

What are the things that God wants you to accomplish but seem too hard? They seem like you can't do them. I encourage you to challenge those areas. Don't accept the lie as the truth. There are countless businesses, books, ministries, marriages, families, and more that have been snuffed out by the lie of "Can't Do It."

From this day forward, I want you to challenge the lie. In every area, in every situation, and every time you feel like you can't do something, tell yourself, "I can do all things through Christ!" Write it on your mirror, put it on your screensaver, put it in your car, on your refrigerator, wherever, somewhere as a reminder that the lie of "I can't do it" is subject to the truth of "I can do all things through Christ."

Questions:

- What things are possible that you think you can't do?
- What plans have you made that are completely reliant on yourself to accomplish? How have those worked out?
- What are the things God wants you to accomplish but seem too hard?

THREE

God Made This Happen

I started writing this book in 2020. For those who remember 2020, you know it was one of the worst years the world has ever seen. The entire world faced a global pandemic, the Coronavirus, aka COVID-19. COVID-19 killed over 350,000 in the United States[1] and infected over five million Americans.[2] The pandemic closed businesses and eviscerated jobs. Churches closed their doors; mental health issues skyrocketed. In addition to the pandemic, racial tension flared across the country. Sparked by the death of George Floyd, an unarmed Black man, which was recorded and exploded on social media, the country was dunked into a cauldron of anger, fear, and a demand for justice. The news of more African American deaths at the hands of law enforcement officers rose to the surface. The situation devolved into protests and (sometimes) violent outbursts.

Many regarded the summer months of 2020 to be the most racially tense year of the century, equal to the traumatic '60s.

In addition to COVID-19 and the racial tension, multiple wildfire in California destroyed nearly four million acres. Homes and lives were lost. The economic impact exceeded $12 billion.[3] The trauma in 2020 continued. The entertainment industry lost a phenomenal young talent when Chadwick Boseman died of cancer at 43.[4] And in the sports industry, sports fans (avid and casual) were devastated by the news of Kobe Bryant's death in a helicopter crash.[5]

And finally at the end of 2020, a contentious presidential election brought sharper focus to a fractured society after a campaign best categorized as "personal."

In my opinion, the biggest challenge in 2020 was finding faith in a good God even while bad things were happening. It was equally hard to help others in their quest. It is hard preaching the Good News of the Gospel while all you see and hear is bad news. And another lie crept into my head: "God made this happen."

Have you ever looked at bad situations, the loss of loved ones, the loss of a job, the challenges of life, and said the same thing?" If so, this chapter is for you. God did not make bad things happen. He is a good God even when bad things are occurring. Let me show you how I came to that conclusion.

The first thing you have to do is deal with your B.S. That's right, you need to handle all of your bad B.S. I even thought about entitling this book, *How to Handle Your B.S.* Your B.S. controls your entire life. It can make life seem more challenging or more peaceful. It stands is at the core of your life – you either have good B.S. or a bad B.S.. What is it? I am glad you asked.

I am talking about your "Belief System." (Fooled you, didn't I?) What is your belief system? What is at the core of your beliefs? What drives your beliefs? Where do you go to find out the answers to the questions of life? Is it Google, YouTube, friends, parents, your school, yourself, or something else? Who you go to and where you find your answers will tell you where your belief system lies. And remember, "If you don't believe in something you will fall for anything."[6]

In the midst of the challenges I faced and the world I saw growing darker, I choose to stand on and to believe in the Word of God. While the news and social media highlighted on all the wrong, death, and decay that was happening, I turned my attention towards the Bible and spent quality time with Jesus. And I discovered something. God was not making these things happen, but He was allowing them to happen because He was going to turn them around and somehow use them for His good. I realized I had to stop trying to make sense of everything and have faith that God was someway using every event to showcase His Glory.

One passage was particularly helpful:

And we know that all things work together for good to those who love God, to those who are the called according to His purpose. (Romans 8:28, New King James Version)

How could bad and hateful things show us how good and loving God is? Again, it comes back to your B.S.. Are you going to believe that all things are working together or decide things are simply falling apart? When you look at the bad things, you can either focus on them or search for the good destined to arise from them.

Dwight L. Moody, the American evangelist, once opined, "The best way to show that a stick is crooked is not to argue about it or to spend time denouncing it, but to lay a straight stick alongside it." To know things are bad, you must know what good looks like – and to recognize good, you need a moral compass. God is our moral compass. He points toward what is right and directs our thinking, our beliefs, and our lives towards His goodness and His purposes.

A job loss, the death of a loved one, losing out on a promotion, longing for a life partner, murder, mayhem, and the evil of this world all point to our nature as broken, sinful people in need of a powerful, loving, and good God. The brokenness of this world shows us how desperately we need a savior to help and to fix.

So did God cause these wrong things to happen?

Absolutely not. The Bible is very clear about the genesis of evil, death and destruction:

> The thief comes only to steal and kill and destroy; I have come that they may have life, and have it to the full. (John 10:10, NIV)

The "thief" is the devil, Satan, or Lucifer. All these names represent different ways to address the evil one.

So, if the devil is doing all the evil, but God is powerful, why doesn't He stop it? This question has been raised countless times over the course of the centuries. I have heard it on numerous occasions as a pastor. While I am not a world famous theologian, I never feel completely qualified to answer this question. I know some things though. While on this side of heaven, somethings are simply a mystery to us. In addition, I know that how God operates and thinks is something far higher and greater than our ability. "God's ways are higher than our ways and His thinking is far beyond ours" (Isaiah 55:8). Nevertheless, I would like to take an opportunity to answer the question, "If God is powerful, why doesn't He stop evil things?"

I believe God allows negative things to happen because by allowing them, He wakes us up. He causes us to see things and be introspective. We find out about our faith, about who we trust, and determine to whom we turn to for comfort and guidance. Negative situations are the perfect opportunity for us to stretch our thinking, strengthen our faith, and readjust priorities in our lives. As it is written:

> My brothers and sisters, when you have many kinds of troubles, you should be full of joy, because you know that these troubles test your faith, and this will give you patience.
> James 1:2-3 New Century Version

It is important to address the lie of "God made this happen." If not, we will go our whole lives thinking we are being punished – or God is trying to hurt us. Negative things come from the devil but God can take any negative and use it for a positive. I don't know what positive it can bring in your life, but God does and He wants to develop you in the trials, strengthen you during the resistance, and refine you in the fire.

I challenge you to ask better questions and to go from, "Why did God do this?" to "Why is God allowing this to happen?" Take it a step further. Ask God, "What are you developing in me?" The answers to the right questions will be what helps you grow. The ability to rejoice and reflect properly in the midst of challenges is a sign of true emotional and spiritual maturity.

I think back on my life. When I was about 11 years old, one Saturday morning I was watching cartoons and eating my cereal. I heard a knock. I opened the door hoping it was my friends asking me to play. To my dismay, it was a host of DEA, FBI, and other law enforcement officers with guns drawn demanding to come into our home! I was afraid – in shock. I wondered if I was having a nightmare. They gathered our whole family in the living room. My father explained to my mom and my other two siblings that he was under investigation because two men from his doctor's office died from an overdose of medication. He reassured us everything was going to be okay. We waited patiently as they ransacked our entire house. The officers even brought out some of my toys and asked what they were and where I got them. When I had to go to the bathroom, one of them stood at the door to watch me pee.

It was horrific, but we tried to remain calm. After a while – it felt like all day – they holstered their weapons, the news helicopters flew away, the yellow crime scene tape disappeared, and things went back to normal.

As we put things back in place, we all felt violated. I couldn't make sense of it. I didn't understand what was happening. There was only so much my 11 year old self could comprehend about the law and how the world worked. All I knew was my Father, a great family physician and a well-known community leader, was being treated like a criminal. The next two years were strange. My father stopped working as a doctor. At one point, he mowed lawns. I didn't ask a lot of questions; I just observed. He never gave us the impression that anything seriously negative was taking place. He made sure out day-to-day operations remained the same. He took me to school, showed up for practices, and made sure I engaged in all my extracurriculars.

For the next two years I carried on about my life as normal, going to school, hanging out with friends, playing in the band, coming home, eating, and being a regular kid. When I was 13, I realized a trial had been going on. In retrospect it made sense why I got certain looks from teachers, deans and my friends' parents. They knew something I didn't. I later learned that my dad's trail made headline news in our city.

As a physician my father had the responsibility, under oath, to do no harm to those he served. Unfortunately, two men came to my father's office had requested help with their lower back pain. At the time, there was new drug designed to alleviate pain. The two men received the drug. Unfortunately, they became addicted. What was intended to be useful sent the two men along a hellish, downward spiral of substance abuse and ultimately death. The law at the time held doctors accountable. So, they arrested my father and put him on trial for the death of these men.

At the end of the trial my father was sentenced to two life sentences in prison. At 13, I didn't understand what was going on, why this was happening, or fully grasp the extent of the trouble my father was in. All I remember was my father who was a great dad, an excellent husband, a phenomenal role model, and a man of God many people admired, was facing the rest of his life in prison.

I wasn't at any of the trails or hearings, for good reasons I suppose. Looking back and talking with my mom, I have pieced together some of what transpired. But during that time, I had no idea. I could only imagine the emotions my father went through when the guilty verdict was given and the sentence was announced. When I heard about it, I was in total disbelief. I was sure it was all a big misunderstanding and everything was going to get cleared up soon. Even when he was sentenced to life in prison, I made up my teenage mind that everything would be fine and he would be out in a couple of days.

A year went by; my father was still in prison. We made regular visits to see him and we spent time talking about life and school. He would come off as if things weren't too bad, fueling my naivety. During our visits, I noticed my father was losing a lot of weight. He said it because of his regular exercise routine and a new diet.

The first job I had was working at a dog kennel, taking care of animals while their owners traveled. They hired me because they needed someone to work the weekends and holidays. I had a lot of availability. However, they asked me to work one Christmas. I told them I couldn't because I planned on seeing my father. The employer said, "If you don't show up for work, don't bother showing up again. We hired you for holidays and we need you for this one." That was the last time I ever spoke to him because we drove to visit my dad. I am thankful we did. Little did I know the trip would be one of the last times I saw him.

My father had lung cancer. He had never smoked a day in his life. We were shocked. I was still grappling with his incarceration; now I found out he was sick.

My father died when I was 15. I was angry. I was confused. I was hurt. I was lost.

I was angry at so many people. I was angry at God. I couldn't understand how He would allow such a terrible thing to happen to my dad. I couldn't put my trust in a God who would do such a thing. Turning to God for comfort was the last thing I wanted to do.

Time went on and I made a lot of mistakes in my early teenage years. I got involved in partying, drinking, and drugs. I didn't have any direction in life and was too angry to listen to advice from the role models I had like my brother, coach, and others. Life was bleak. I was going through the motions, just doing what I had to do to get by, but there wasn't true purpose or motivation. I graduated from high school by the grace of God but about a month after graduation, I got arrested for a high-speed chase with the police. It was my first offense. I had just turned 18, so they cut me some slack and gave me a pretty light sentence that involved probation. I had an opportunity to go to college, so I moved from my hometown to go to a public college in Gainesville, Florida.

Although my surroundings and environment changed, my habits didn't. I made the same mistakes with bad behavior. I even had another run in with the police, but managed not to get caught. Lucky for me; I was on probation and would have gotten in a lot of trouble.

I kept pushing the limits. I guess I thought I was above the law. Deep down, however, I had a feeling that perhaps my "grace period" was running out. I was very close to making a life alerting mistake. Looking back now, I know the Holy Spirit was trying to get my attention. What happened next changed everything for me.

One night in college, after leaving a night club, I ran into some folks from my church in the club parking lot. They were praying with people. Someone approached me and asked if I had a relationship with God. I said, "I heard about Him before in Vacation Bible School." "Do you think you are close in your relationship with Jesus?" they asked. Immediately I felt convicted. It was like life flashed before my eyes. I realized the reason I was partying, drinking, sleeping around, and living the "college" lifestyle was because I was trying to numb the pain of losing my father. I needed to fill the God-sized hole in my heart.

Their next question was, "Do you want to rededicate your life to Jesus?" My answer was, "Yes." I didn't get all the answers I needed right then. I still harbored anger towards God, but I knew I needed to take a step in another direction. They invited me to church the following Sunday. I went. This was where I was called to the ministry...where I met my wife...where we started a family...where I served on staff as a youth pastor...and where I attend today!

Through prayer and great relationships with pastors and leaders in my church, is where I came to understand how

God allows negative things – and how he uses them for His glory.

Pain is real. I am not diminishing the anger, hurt, or grief you feel. I cannot imagine what you may have experienced or the anguish you endure. I do not want to be insensitive to your experiences. Instead, I want to help shift your perspective so you can see your pain, anguish, loss, heartache, or any other negative circumstance the same way God sees it.

Here is what I concluded to the question: Is God a good God, *even if* bad things happen?

1) Life is difficult: Our Pastor teaches a principle he learned from his therapist. It is simple but mind-blowing. Pastor Ken told this therapist all the hard things he was facing and the difficult issues he faced. He expected sympathy. He didn't get it. The therapist said, "Do you know what your problem is? Your problem is you haven't accepted the fact that life is difficult." Often times we have a fairytale picture of life and think that everything will be happily ever after. But the truth is, life is difficult. Yes, the majority of life is filled with great moments, exciting times, and all sorts of fulfilling things. However, if we expect life always to be "happy, happy, joy, joy, we will be blindsided by difficulty. Expect life to be hard. Just because there are obstacles does not mean God is absent. In fact, God tells us there will be trouble of all kinds in this world and encourages us to take

heart, because he has overcome the world! So settle in your heart. The goodness of God never changes.

2) Things Above our Understanding: When my daughter was young, she loved to play in my car. With the car off and parked in the garage and the keys far away, she would turn on the lights, push the flasher button, and play with the locks. One day, she asked if she could drive. We told her "No" and got the standard kid response: "Why?" I told her she was too young. "Why?" This kept up for a while until I brought "the hammer": "Because that is the way God designed things." When it comes to processing hard things and understanding the goodness of God even in hardship, we sometimes have to accept the same answer: "That is the way God designed things." One thing I learned over the years, "When intellect ends, faith starts." Many times we want an explanation for why things happen. However, the justified explanation can sometimes keep us from exercising our faith and trusting that God is in full control and working things out! I love what Isaiah says:

> *For my thoughts are not your thoughts,*
> *neither are your ways my ways,"*
> *declares the Lord.*
> *As the heavens are higher than the earth,*
> *so are my ways higher than your ways*
> *and my thoughts than your thoughts.*

In this life on Earth, we have to accept one fact: there are simply some things we will not understand. Is that an excuse not to grow in your understanding? Absolutely not. You can seek understanding, knowledge, and insight, but on occasion, we must ask, "When is enough – enough?" At what point will you feel satisfied in your understanding? If we eventually come to the conclusion that there are things above our understanding, we'll travel down a never-ending black hole. We will seek to fill a space with knowledge that can only be filled with faith!

3) Never Bring God Down to Your Level of Circumstances: Lecrae is one of my favorite artists. I have been listening to his music since middle school. In one of his songs, "Hammer Time," he says, "You don't measure up, I met the ruler." He is referencing God and his standard of measurement compared to how we (including what we go through) don't align. (This includes the things we endure and encounter in life.) I love this because it's so true. God's standard of measurement is different from ours! We often look at bad situations and put ourselves in God's position of making judgments, conclusions, and even attempting to control situations. In doing so, we think we know what is right as if we hold the measuring stick of life. We look at what happens to us and what happens to others. By employing our limited understanding, we determine what is fair, right, and acceptable. If we want to have a better understanding of life's most difficult situations, we must allow God to be the one who judges, controls, and has the final say. If we look at our situations and think that God can't handle them, we're mistaken. Instead of looking at your problem and allowing it to tell

how bad things are, look to God and remind your problem how big He is.

4) God is Good and Works Everything For His Good: There is a popular verse that many Christians like to quote, but sometimes is hard for us to believe and accept.

And we know that all things work together for good to them that love God, to them who are the called according to his purpose. (Romans 8:28)

What makes this passage hard to believe and accept is imagining how *all thigs work together for good*, even the most tragic, traumatic, and worst situations of life. Here is where we face a challenge. God's word is either 100% right or 100% wrong. I don't know about you, but I'd rather believe His word is 100% right. So what does that mean for us? To believe that all things are working together for God, we need to find out what "good" is, because if His word is true, there has to be something! Here are some questions designed to help us find the good. What event or situation comes to your mind that is difficult to process? Now with that in mind, ask yourself the following questions:

- What is God developing in me from this situation?
- How can Jesus be glorified in this situation?
- How did Jesus handle a situation similar to this?
- Who can I help with my testimony of overcoming this?

The heart behind these questions is believing there is something good and knowing we must look for it. Often times in the trials and pains of life, instead of looking for the good, all we have our eyes fixated on is the bad. We ask, "Why did this bad thing happen? Why does this hurt? Why does life have to be this painful?" But if you ask the above questions, they can change your frame of mind and ultimately your heart to look for something good out of it.

5) Death is a Gift: Yes, that's right. Dying is a gift to us. Now take a breath, adjust your eyebrows and relax. If you're anything like me and were confused when you first read the sentence, allow me to explain. I have learned over the years, that God will offend your mind so He can reveal your heart. The idea of death is not a pleasant thought – definitely not something we view as a gift. However, as believers in Jesus, we carry in our hearts the understanding of life's temporary nature. We pass through it on the way to heaven with our Heavenly Father. The only way to live forever in heaven is to die here on earth. It was not always supposed to be that way. When God created Adam and Eve, He intended them live forever and know no death. They were to live forever in the Garden with God. This is a picture of what heaven looks like. When they ate the forbidden fruit, they sinned and separated themselves from God. God banished them from the Garden because there could be no sin in God's presence. God then set up two angels to guard Eden to ensure sin would not enter.

When Jesus came to Earth, everything changed. By believing in Jesus, our sins are forgiven and we gain access to God's presence and to Heaven. Jesus, who did not sin, died so that we who are sinners can live (eternally).We are destined for paradise , something not of this natural Earth. To get there, we must die. Death, a gift, allows us to be with God forever without sin, pain, sorrow, or sickness. You see, we no longer need to fear death. We don't have to be sad when a loved one passes away, because to be absent from the body is to be present with the Lord (2 Corinthians 5:8)!

FOUR

I Don't Have Enough _____

There's a story of a husband and wife who got upset over their neighbors hanging "dirty" clothes in their backyard. One morning the wife was washing dishes and looked out of the kitchen window. She saw the neighbors laughing and hanging seemingly dirty clothes on the clothing line. She said to her husband, "Babe, can you believe this, the neighbors hung up dirty clothes on the clothing line in their backyard." The husband looked, chuckled, and when on about his day. The next day the wife was in the kitchen again and saw dirty clothes hanging on the clothesline. She called to her husband and said, "Do you see this, they have dirty clothes on the clothes line *again*! We better say something, that's nasty." The husband chuckled again and the wife got upset. "Why do you think that is so funny? Aren't you going to say something to them?" He shrugged his shoulders and went on about his day. On the next day, the wife was relieved. She looked out the window and saw there were not any dirty clothes hanging up outside. She called to her husband and said, "It's about time, the neighbors finally cleaned their dirty clothes." He chuckled and said, "No sweetheart, they didn't clean their dirty clothes, I just cleaned our dirty window."

I wonder how many times in our life the dirty perspectives we look though determines the dirt we see. So many of the decisions we make, the things we say, and the conclusions we come up with in our mind are determined by a wrong perspective. The lie we often tell ourselves (because of a wrong perspective) is: "I don't have enough." This lie has kept many people from achieving their God given dreams: the lie of "I don't have enough time, money, energy, knowledge, or any other resource." But the truth is, you have all you need. We need to shift our perspective. It's not a matter of what you have, it's a matter of what you do with what you have.

In John 6, Jesus asks his disciples to get food to feed five thousand people. His disciples scoff and say (in essence); "No way. We don't have enough money" to buy food for these people. Jesus takes five loaves of bread and two small fish and miraculously feeds everyone. The story points to God's ability to take the small amounts we have to do big things. Not only was he able to feed five thousand people, but there were also leftovers.

I wonder how many people could benefit from your gifts and talents if you simply used what you have. If you wait to start until the day when you "have enough," you will never begin. You will get more as you begin than you had before you started. We can't wait until the "perfect" conditions before we begin. Even the Bible mentions that (Ecclesiastes 11:4). Unfortunately, too many people fall prey to the lie of "I don't have enough" and simply never start.

But not you. You are going to give it all you have with all you got because you already have everything you need to succeed. If there is something you want to accomplish, you can do it. Take the little you have and start! It may not look like you want it to now, but don't let that stop you. Soon enough, you will realize your dream is you keep going!

My wife and I always wanted to travel to Los Angeles. We'd watch movies and see TV shows about LA and I would tell her, "Baby, one day when we have enough money, I am going to take you to there." Little did I know all I needed was nine dollars.

One day out of the blue my pastor called me and said, "Hey I going to preach in LA, do you want to come with me?" We found a babysitter, packed our bags and next thing I knew, we were on a flight from Orlando, FL. to Los Angeles, California. All the expenses we paid for, hotel, travel, and food. The only thing we paid for was a $9 meal on the flight. Good thing because we surely did not have enough on our own.

I wonder what you could achieve, the things you could do. and the places you could go if you rejected the lie of "I don't have enough." Take the little you have and reach for your big dream.

This is a hard concept to understand for a lot of people and counter to what we continually hear. You need to have "this degree" before you start a career or "that title" before you become a leader. You need a spouse before you can feel loved. The list never ends.

We have the tendency to look at what we don't have" before we see what we do. If you are not careful, all you will see is what you can't do and miss what you can.

God uses small things to make something big. In fact, God watches over how we use the small things to determine if He will give us larger things.

> Whoever can be trusted with very little can also be trusted with much, and whoever is dishonest with very little will also be dishonest with much. (Luke 16:10 NIV)

How we steward the small things in our lives will determine how we handle the big things. Unfortunately, way too many people disqualify themselves for much because they are mishandling or missing the little of what they have. Here are some ways I think we can see the potential in whatever we have.

1. Gratitude. One of the things we can get from the story of Jesus feeding five thousand people is that He was grateful. He thanked God for the "two-

piece dinner" on hand and He blessed it. What God did from there was a miracle. We should look at the things we have and be grateful for them. They may not be the thing we want, but we can be thankful because there are some people with far less. You have a job? Be grateful. You have money? Be grateful. You have breath, a family, eyes to see, ears to hear, legs on which to walk? Be grateful. I do two things designed to bolster my gratitude.

2. I wake up every morning and say: "This is the best day of my life! I am grateful for the breath God put in my lungs!"

3. I write a "grateful journal," where I record at least three things for which I am grateful everyday

We all have something for which to be grateful. In fact, we have a lot, but gratitude requires intentionality – focus. Remember, our culture zeros in on what we are lacking. Push back on the sentiment.

When I began my grateful journal, it was pretty shallow. I wrote down things like coffee, clean clothes, and cereal. (Eventually, I moved past the "C's." haha) But I kept at it. Now, I record phone calls with leaders with over ten years of ministry experience, my loving and supportive wife (who should have been listed first), potty training for our daughter. Taking the time to write down specific items – large or small – puts them front and center in my prayers and in my life.

1. Faithfulness. This one is huge. Being faithful over

whatever you have is one of the biggest avenues leading to an understanding of the miracles God continues to work. He is always taking note of how we use the gifts we have and how faithful we are with them. Practically speaking, that means taking care of the things you have: your car, clothes, house, etc. We have the tendency to want something nicer, bigger, or more effective, faithfulness requires us to consider how we treat what we already have. How well have you taken care of the current car? Do you wash it? Are you diligent about hanging up and laundering the clothes you have? You want a big house? What does your apartment look like?

When my pastor first married, he and his spouse were in their early twenties. Their combined income was fourteen thousand a year. They shared their apartment with roaches and mice; the drove a beater. The sideview mirror was broken and the roof leaked. But they didn't look at what they had and say, "We don't have enough." Instead, they started calling their car a "Mercedes Benz" and their apartment a "mansion." And they treated them as such. The apartment was immaculate; the car was always clean. In seven short years, their income exceeded seven hundred thousand.

I am *not* saying that being faithful will make you a near millionaire, but I promise God will honor your faithfulness towards the little you have and build on it. What might your life look like if you dedicated yourself to being faithful over whatever you have?

2. Imagination. Our imagination is a powerful gift from God. If I describe something, I am sure you could see it without physically seeing it. Imagine a black SUV driving down a road. Can you see it? Now imagine it changing color from black to yellow. Let the vehicle morph into a red sports car getting pulled over by the police. Can you see it?

"Seeing" the car didn't take too much effort, did it? And it was probably fun. But we were considering something positive. Sometimes we let out imaginations wander into dark places and then it becomes burdensome. Our lives often follow our imaginations. If you see yourself failing, you may, indeed, fail. We have the God-given ability to image our futures.

When you imagine positive things – success, achievement, growing old with your spouse, children, and grandchildren – these events can come to pass. If we are intentional, we can use our imagination to see the things we want to become and achieve.

In Richard Foster's book, *Celebration of Discipline*, he writes: "We believe He [God] can sanctify the imagination and use it for His good purposes" (Foster, p. 26).

Casting down imaginations, and every high thing that exalteth itself against the knowledge of God, and bringing into captivity every thought to the obedience of Christ. II Corinthians 10:5

The challenge we face is to align our thoughts and dreams with God and His purposes. We need to imagine the things God wants us to imagine. Be assured, God wants you to imagine taking the little you have and trusting Him to do something exceedingly, abundantly *above* what you can think or imagine (Ephesians 3:20). What could your "little" look like if you took it and imagined it was something greater?

3. Giving. Generosity is the antidote to selfishness and doubt. When you give to others (and more importantly to God), it is doing something in your heart. God doesn't want your money; God wants your heart. And when you give to God, you move your heart in the direction God desires. In Matt. 6:21, it talks about "where your treasure is, there your heart will be also." If you want to know someone's priorities, look at their budget. If you want to know where people put their hope and trust, pay attention to where their money goes first. When we give, we exhibit our trust in God. When we tithe, giving the first ten percent to God, we express our belief in His ability to do more with ten percent than we can do with ninety.

Go back to the story of the loaves and fish. Imagine the boy's response when Jesus decided to use that small meal to feed the large crowd. Put yourself in the kid's shoes. He probably had plans for that food. Perhaps he was on his way home to give the food to his family. Maybe he worked all day for it. Maybe he was an orphan and this was the only meal he had for the day. We do not know anything except that he *gave* what he had to Jesus. He put His trust in Jesus. One sure way to change the perspective of what you have being enough is by giving to God and trusting Him turn your little into a lot.

From this day forward, I extend this challenge. Don't look at what you have and think it's not enough. God can take what you have (regardless of the amount) and turn it into something far beyond your imagination. All you have is all you need. God will do the rest.

Now, let's get to work.

Questions:

- "I don't have enough _____." What do you fill in the blank with?
- What can you do to see protentional in what you do have?
- What of the things you imagine you are missing do you think God can increase?

FIVE

If That Hadn't Happened, I Would Be Farther Along By Now

Have you ever gotten lost? Perhaps you were on your way to a destination, excited to get there, and somehow, something happened and you ended up somewhere else. Maybe you were frustrated, mad, or upset, or maybe you were intrigued. Perhaps your unintended locale was interesting and you enjoyed seeing new sights and a new environment. You probably got to your original destination eventually, but not before enduring what a lot of people encounter every day. Plans don't always go the way we wanted; things turn out unexpectedly; people don't do or act as we had hoped. Let's call these "detours." Can you believe that all your detours ultimately lead to your destiny? Whatever happened (or didn't happen) might not have been in your plans, but God can still use our "detours" in life to reach His plan and His glory for your life.

During my last year of college at the University of Florida I experienced one of the biggest detours of my life. It was the final stretch. I had one semester to go. I only needed four more classes to graduate. Things looked good. My wife (then my fiancé) and I were planning a wedding. We had agreed we would graduate from college before we got married. Classes begin and I walked into class day after day, head held high, ready to take on the world. Nothing was going to stop me! The semester got off to a great start. All of my classes were fairly easy, except for one, Modern Greek.

That's right, for my foreign language requirement, I decided to take Modern Greek during my final semester. I had a fantastic teacher. She was patient, relatable, personable, and believed the best in all of her students. The first test went well. It was simple memorization of the Greek alphabet. The second test was on basic words – simple memorization, but I didn't do as well. By the last test of the semester, something wasn't right. I had applied my regular study techniques. I was working with study buddies and visiting my teacher for help, but I didn't understand the material. As much as I tried, I couldn't put my finger on the problem, It felt like my brain wasn't working. Something wasn't clicking; I wasn't firing on all cylinders.

I got frustrated. When I took the final test, I failed miserably. Something was wrong. I went to the Disability Resource Center and I sat down with a phycologist. After intensive testing, it was revealed that I have the inability to decode words of my native language properly, which explained why

I was bombing Greek. I also have an attention deficit disorder.

So, it was the last semester of my college career and I was diagnosed with two major learning disabilities. I wondered why no one had caught these sooner. In addition, I was worried about not graduating, which meant not getting married.

A friend shared an audio book entitled *David and Goliath* by Malcolm Gladwell. The book focused on the probability of improbable events occurring in situations where one outcome is greatly favored over the other. It was a revelation. And it seemed like every part of the book dealt exactly with what I was going through. I remember driving to class one day, the one where I was struggling. Questions pounded in my head: "What am I going to do?" "Should I keep moving forward?" "Why am I even going to class?"

In one place, Gladwell said, "an extraordinary amount of highly successful people are diagnosed with a learning disability." He quoted a study by Julie Logan from City University, London where she states, "the number of CEOs who are diagnosed with a learning disability is one third." Malcolm wrote: "In some extraordinary cases, difficulties cause people to think more deeply about whatever they come across. The difficult situation requires the person to overcome insecurity and humiliation, focus hard and have the panache to put on a successful performance."[1] It's what he calls the "Desirable Difficulty." It felt like Gladwell had been spying on my life.

I could not believe my ears. I replayed and re-listened to that part of the book at least ten times. I had a rush of emotions – a release, a charge of energy. I was shocked, overjoyed, and confused. The perspective of my challenge changed. I went from believing my struggle was holding me back to understanding my struggle was helping to push me forward.

We often look at the set back as something prohibiting us from moving forward. We say, "If this didn't happen to me, if things didn't go this way, if they wouldn't have left my life, I would have gotten the job. If this person didn't die, if I wasn't sick, I would be farther along." But I want to challenge your thinking.

You are where you need to be. The mess is creating a message. The challenge you faced will help you become better in the future. Your best days are still ahead of you because nothing can stop God from producing the goodness's inside of you. All of your detours can lead to God's destiny for your life. If you're still breathing, He still has a plan for you. If you're not dead, God's not done!

> He cuts off every branch in me that bears no fruit, while every branch that does bear fruit he prunes so that it will be even more fruitful. (John 15:2)

Did you catch that? Whether you are producing fruit or not, God is trimming you, pruning you to be better. You have to get this in your spirit. God is using every obstacle, every challenge, to trim you to be even more fruitful. You can look at your situation as a setback or look at it as a set up − a set up to be better, to be stronger, to lean on God more, to be more fruitful. God's heart for us is to be as fruitful as we possibly can. But He allows us to go through seasons, circumstances, and changes that often don't feel fruitful at all. They are simply pruning seasons designed to make us more fruitful than we can imagine.

In Chapter 3, I talked about my father going to prison and dying when I was 15 years old. I couldn't believe what was going on. I was numb to the pain and acted nonchalantly about the situation. My anger and sadness expressed themselves in making wrong decisions about who I hung out with, what I did on the weekends, and the lifestyle I lived. I viewed what happened to my father as a huge set back in my life. I thought I wouldn't become much of anything. I didn't have much positive motivation to do great things, if anything, for God. I was distant from God. I had a hole in my hearth and I attempted to fill it with lustful desires and the things of this world. Each time, they left me wanting more because they promised only temporary healing. I was drinking, smoking, and being involved in promiscuous things almost every weekend between the ages of sixteen and eighteen.

After graduating high school, I got into more trouble as I mentions. I continued misbehaving in Gainesville. Many who were looking from afar saw a young man whose life was not going nowhere. I am sure it looked like there was no hope for me. I was a disappointment to many people – they thought I was wasting my life.

It all changed on Easter weekend. I went to a night club with some "friends" of mine, a regular thing. I was usually the hype man when we went out; I always had good time. But that evening was different. I didn't feel the same. I wasn't the hype man; I was the mad man. I didn't want to dance, didn't want to be there, and I had a bad attitude. I almost picked a fight with a bouncer and they told me to leave. I was half drunk.

As I wrote earlier, some folks from my church were praying for people outside. When one of them approached, I thought he was *Prayer at two in the morning – outside a bar?* But when he asked me if I knew Jesus, everything changed. I felt a tug on my heart to repent. It was almost like my whole life had been leading up to that moment. I gave my life to Christ outside of a night club in the wee hours of the morning. They invited me to Church. I went and have been there ever since.

When I got plugged in and began attending church on a regular basis, my relationship with God began to flourish. I started sensing a call to become a pastor. I spoke to my pastor about it. He said, "Great, you want to be a pastor, start pastoring." He gave me the six-month challenge. He told me to give God six months – to go all in for half a year and see what God would do. He told me to give, pray, attend regularly, serve, and get connected in community. He encouraged me by saying, "Seasons can change in six months and so can your life." So I did. I adjusted areas of my life to make sure I could go all in for God for six months and I began to realize the power of God working in a short period of time. I changed my friend group, I started growing in my faith drastically, I began reading the Bible, I got a promotion in my job, and, most importantly I received peace, direction, and clarity in my life.

Part of me was excited about my walk with God. I understood more clearly what God called me to do. However, another part of me was frustrated because I wondered where my life could have been if I had started the six-month challenge sooner. Could my life be farther along?

Many of us look in the mirror and reflect on our lives. We often want to change. We want things to be bigger, smaller, faster, slower, taller, shorter, quicker, or whatever. We were born to see things change. When Adam and Eve were created, God said, "Be fruitful and multiply." On the inside, all of us have an internal motivator. It challenges us. It makes us question what we do or where we are. This can be both good and bad. In a good instance, our thoughts drive us to be more successful and push us to grow. On the flip side, the same sentiment can make us feel inadequate, like we are not good enough or unsuccessful. It can lead to frustration, disappointment, or discouragement.

After six months, I was faced with a decision to make. I was either going to choose, "I should be farther along than I am," or "I am right where I need to be." Maybe some of you are in the same place. You think you aren't where you're supposed to be. You imagine if things had been different in the past, you would be somewhere different now or in the future. Although the thinking sounds logical, there is a choice involved. Are you going to insist you have missed it or will you believe that everything lead you to God's destiny for your life?

I could have easily looked at my life and claimed I would have been a doctor if my dad hadn't gone to jail. I might have attended a different college if I hadn't wasted my high school days. I would have been smarter if my dad had not died when I was a young person. But I now believe God took full control of my life once I surrendered my will to Him and He re-directed my life to follow my destiny no matter what happened in the past. I am exactly where I need to be and doing exactly what I need to be doing.

Here are some practical ways to get where you need to be.

1. Accept It

One of the most frustrating things in life is trying to change un-changeable things. We chase happiness and a stress-free, problem free life. In reality, life throws us curveballs. Nothing is stress-free or without problems. Life is difficult – accept it. Things do not always go according to plan. My pastor said it this way. "If you are fighting your whole life trying to make life 'happy.' you will be frustrated when you never reach it." Accepting life as difficult, problem prone, and unpredictable will give you a better perspective when it comes to understanding where you are.

2. Don't Compare

Comparison is one of the biggest enemies to our success in life. If we are too focused on what others are doing, we will miss what we're supposed to be doing. Ever noticed the blinders they put on race horses? It blocks their peripheral vision. If they see the other horses next to them, thoroughbreds will run slower, which can cause them to lose. Some of us are way too concerned about the people running alongside. We are too busy looking at what they are doing. We compare where we are to where they claim to be. It can be discouraging. Blind yourself to the distractions and comparisons of life and focus on what you are supposed to be doing. Reject the lies that accompany comparison.

3. Challenge Your Thoughts

Have you ever had a thought that sounded one way in your head but ridiculous when you said it aloud? That happens to me probably on a daily basis. I am notorious at speaking before I think. I am working on the issue. The thoughts I have in my head are often inaccurate. When I articulate them, I realize how outlandish they are. My thoughts will run wild and suggest all sorts of negativity. I don't know about you, but my thoughts have the tendency to run wild like a runaway train – just going, going, going until it ultimately crashes and explodes into a flame of confusion, discouragement, and fear. It's not until I am intentional about saying to myself, "That's a bad thought; I rebuke it in the name of Jesus," that I am able to control the runaway train of thought. If you want to have the right perspective on where you are in life, challenge every thought that suggests that we aren't where you need to be. Sometimes we need to other people to challenge our thoughts. I often go to someone I trusted and asked "Hey, what do you think about this, I was thinking…" More than occasionally, they tell me I should be aiming in the opposite direction.

4. Keep Going

We all fail, we all make mistakes, and we all have setbacks. But what keeps us from abject failure is what we do when we run into a problem. Anyone with any sort of success in life will tell you they have failed multiple times. But they look at their failure, learn from it, and keep going. No matter what setback you've had in life, you have to keep going. Maybe you're in a good place right now, no failures, no real challenges – great! Make a decision to keep going even if you run into a figurative wall. If you've been knocked down, get back up! Figure out what happened and do better the next time. Michael Jordan said, "I've missed more than 9000 shots in my career. I've lost almost 300 games. Twenty-six times I've been trusted to take the game winning shot and missed. I've failed over and over and over again in my life... that is why I succeed."

From this day forward, I hope you will begin to realize that God has you where you are on purpose and for a purpose. The lies of "what if" and "could have been" are behind you. From now on, you are going to keep moving forward with a perspective that you can and will do great things no matter your past, challenges, failures, or setbacks!

Questions:

- What setbacks do you think you have faced?
- How can you see protentional in what you do have?
- How can God help you to increase your potential?

SIX

I Need a Sign

People who live on purpose live for their purpose. In other words, when we know what you're purposed to do, we often have a better direction, motivation, and drive for our lives. People who have not yet had their purpose revealed to them tend to go through life haphazardly or go through the motions. On the contrary, people who know their purpose typically wake up early, achieve goals, and seem almost immune to the effects of negativity. They are living their lives knowing what they are supposed to do, their purpose.

Jon Gordon in his book, *The Power of Positive Leadership*, says: "We don't get burned out because of what we do. We get burned out when we forget why we do it." When we know why we do something, the purpose behind what we do, we have more strength, power and motivation to achieve things. But what about the people who don't know their purpose?

What about people who don't know what they are supposed to do?

I have been there before – not knowing what I was "purposed" to do. I used to get intimidated by the words "purpose" or "calling." To me those were things I didn't understand. I assumed God would show me something as important as a purpose. I figured big things arrived through a dream, or clouds spelling out the words in the sky, or the stars aligning at night, or the audible voice of God. I assumed everyone who knew their purpose had some large "sign" in life, something to point the way.

While that might be true for some people, I have some to realize it is not always the case. Most of us discover our purpose through various life events. Over time it becomes clearer as we move closer to it.

Here are some ways I have seen my purpose revealed in my life. I am not saying these are the only ways, nor am I claiming these will be the exact ways your purpose will be revealed to you. These are simply how I believe my calling was revealed to me. Hopefully, you will find some inspiration and encouragement for you to discover your purpose as well.

Slowly

When I am hungry and I have the choice between a microwavable dinner or a slow roasted chicken, I will usually reach for the quicker choice. It is easy, fast, and doesn't leave mess for me to clean up. The same often proves true where are looking for our purpose.

We live in a "microwave generation." We want things fast and when we want them. We hate to wait. Buffering, long lines, extensions, hold times, etc. are experiences we do not like. We want expedited, fast, instant, express, etc.

The word "slow" sounds like a curse in the 21st century. We don't want slow Wi-Fi, slow traffic, slow responses to a text message or email, or slow lines at the store or amusement park. Everything needs to be fast. Consequently, many businesses pride themselves on selling you something that enables you to do whatever you need it fast. Think about it. When you listen to ads, how often do they mention how "fast" they can do something? My favorite are the weight loss commercials where you can lose weight nearly overnight.

We want everything at microwave speed. Press a couple of buttons, wait a minute – poof! But sometimes God wants us to simmer…to slow down…to be deliberate. He likes things to marinate, cook slowly, get tender. He wants things to finish at the right time – to taste better. He understands how complex, important matters do not happen overnight. So, He reveals our purpose slowly.

Day by day, week by week, month by month, year by year God is preparing us, getting us ready, tenderizing us, and showing us our purpose. Can it come overnight? Absolutely. Can it take decades? Yes. Everyone's timeline for their purpose is different, but through it all, God remains close. More than knowing your purpose God wants you to know Him. If you feel like your purpose is taking too long to develop, consider how close you are with God. How strong is your relationship? The deeper the relationship grows, the sooner you will have your purposed revealed.

Secretly

"God whispers, but the devil yells." Ever heard the expression? I believe it is true, especially when it comes to knowing what God is asking for us to do, our purpose. There are so many loud distractions in this world – thousands of things demand our attention and distract us from hearing God. We have deadlines to meet at work, responsibilities at home, personal goals we are trying to reach, expectations from friends and family – and everyone is yelling at the same time.

I am not saying your goals are from the devil or your family is sent from hell. But, the devil will use distractions to keep us from walking in our true calling and purpose. The word "distraction" simply means "to be pulled apart." In Ancient Rome, executioners used distraction as a term to describe death by dismemberment. They would tie a person's arms and legs to four different horses and have the horse pull in four different directions. This s became known as death by "dis-traction."

Many of us are having our life, our attention, our purpose, and our calling ripped apart because so many things demand our attention and we cannot hear from God concerning our purpose. But God is still speaking, leading, and guiding. If you want to hear the purpose God has for you, get to a place where you are quiet and free of distractions. Grab a note pad and a pen. Ask God to speak and begin to write. You may hear nothing at all at first or you may write a whole book, I don't know. But I know God wants to speak to you about your purpose, and we need to make room for Him to speak.

After you have written a few things down (or a whole bunch) consider this: Does my purpose or what God is asking me to do seem possible by myself? If the answer is, "yes," you might not have found your purpose. Allow me to explain.

Often times, the things God want us to do seem impossible of we try them alone. If we can do whatever we think God intends without any help, the task is probably not from God. The Bible tells us we need others in our lives to achieve what God wants to do. (See: Gen. 2:18, II Cor. 12:20-27) It also tells us that what seems impossible to man, is possible for God (Matt. 19:26). If God is purposing us to do something, we will probably think it is impossible or unachievable. That is exactly where God wants us to be, in a place of complete dependence on Him and not relying on ourselves for success.

When God first spoke to me about being a youth pastor, I knew I was supposed to be leading, doing something bigger with my life, and making an impact on others. I knew I was called to lead in some capacity, but I had no idea what it was. One day, my pastor, asked me if I wanted to be a youth pastor. I said, "No. I don't think I would be good. I don't have what it takes and I wouldn't be good with young people." Undeterred, he said, "Okay, no problem, thanks for letting me know." The conversation ended.

I went home and prayed. The Lord whispered to me. "I have called you to pastor. That's it. Whether it is adults, kids, White people, Black people, people in the parking lot, or anyone else, I have called you to pastor, period." I called my pastor the next day and told him, "I am sorry, my answer should have been yes before you even asked. I am called to pastor and if you need a youth pastor, that is what I'll do." The next year was one of the roughest of my life. I had no idea what I had signed myself up for and had absolutely no idea what I was doing. I doubted my call almost every week and wanted to quit almost every day. But looking back, I wouldn't change my time for anything in the world, because when I was dealing with the hardship of my new responsibility, I would get into my quiet time with God, get on my knees asking God to help me, and He would whisper to me, "You have what it takes. Greater is in you than he who is in the world. You can do all things through Christ who gives you the strength. Nothing is too hard for the Lord."

In those quiet moments, God was secretly developing me into the man I am now. If it were not for my season of doubt, I would never have looked toward God and trusted in His ability through me.

If God did it for me, He can do it for you. If there is something God is calling and purposing you to do, I want to encourage you. It may seem impossible to you, but what is impossible to you is possible for God. In the moments when you think there is no way to move forward, just like someone sharing a secret in your ear, God will whisper to you and remind you that you have what it takes and you can do it. It is okay if you have a few doubts; God is bigger than your doubts. Ask Him to help you with your doubts. In fact, your doubts prove you may be doing exactly what God is asking. Think about it. The opposite of certainty is faith. If you were certain about what God has called you to do, you do not need faith. Whenever you have a little doubt, faith fills the gap.

Keep taking steps towards your purpose, keep moving forward, even when it doesn't make sense, even when you can't see it, even when you have doubts, even when it seems impossible or you are afraid, because as you continue to take steps and walk by faith, God is developing your purpose and you will find exactly what He is calling you to do! It may seem like a secret now, but keep taking walking and God will soon reveal to you exactly what you are called and purposed to do!

Subtly

I love watching movies and TV shows with my wife. It's one of the things we do for date nights. One of our favorite TV shows involves a rookie police officer who starts a law enforcement career in his late 40s after a divorce and a near death experience in a bank. He was at the bank when a robbery took place and he found himself staring at the barrel of a gun. Feeling like he had nothing to live for, he jeopardized his own life to save others by taking down the bank robber and saving the day, un-harmed. Afterward, he had an epiphany. He was meant to be a police officer. While the story is exciting, motivating, and makes for great primetime TV, it's not quite how the majority of us find our purpose. Sometimes our purpose comes delicately, low-key, or subtly. Most likely, you are developing in your purpose so quietly that you don't even realize it. Many times we are walking out our purpose every day and never notice it.

If you want to discover what comes naturally to you, take time in your day to be more aware of the things you do, the things you say, and the way you feel. When you hear a friend struggling, do you instantly call or text without thinking or asking, "Why?" Is your purpose to help the hurting and bring restoration to the broken? When you're out and about and you start taking pictures or videos of the things around you, is it because your purpose is possibly to be in the creative arts and media? When your friends and family come to you on a regular basis and ask questions about life, faith, and relationships and you help guide them, maybe you're called to lead, direct, shepherd, teach, or pastor.

Whatever your purpose is, most likely you're already doing something related every day and you don't notice it. Start taking note of the things you're doing and ask why you are doing them. Why do these people come to me? Why do I automatically start doing that? Why do I find myself in this situation? By you asking those questions, you will uncover your purpose – and it will be more evident than you ever suspected.

There's an old saying, "You most likely have never been bitten by an elephant; more likely you've been bitten by a mosquito." It's often the small little things we don't see, don't realize, or come to a surprise that have an effect on us. The same is true with our purpose. It can be right in front of us but because it seems so small or insignificant, we don't see it. Let's open our eyes and see what God has for our lives!

Strategically

There are a great many available resources. I was talking to an older gentlemen in our church one day. Something he said struck me. "Never before have we had access to so much information at our fingertips. We can Google anything and look up whatever we want whenever we want." He was talking about the opportunity we have to access and research information from our phones. We have a connection to the entire world in our pockets or on our desks. Scientists say the iPhone 6 is 32,600 times faster than the computer used to land the Apollo spacecraft on the moon. We have so much information available to us to learn, grow, and develop our purpose, but the question is – do we take advantage of it? I've learned a few things about developing purpose. (Yes, I used Google.) We need to take the time to assess ourselves and find out what makes us tick, what are we good at, and what do we enjoy doing. There are all sorts of free and paid resources available. We can use Strength Finders, High5 tests, Spiritual Gift Assessments, and more. Another way to help figure out our purpose is understanding our values. If you have never taken the opportunity to think through your personal values and write them down, do it. Think about the unchanging things in your life – what cannot be taken away – the lines you will not cross. In *Peak Performances* by Brad Stulberg and Steve Magness, they walk readers through an exercise that helps you with defining your purpose. Below is a brief explanation of how it works.

- Choose 5-7 adjectives that describe your purpose: commitment, community, enthusiasm, inspiration , honor, relationships, loyalty, security, spirituality, or reputation.
- Personalize those core values and explain them and how they apply to your lives. For example: Community – helping people feel included, heard, and having a place to belong.

- Rank your core values. The first being the most important.
- Write out your purpose statement. I came up with, "Building positive relationships with people and helping them find and grow in their purpose through helping them find and grow in God."
- Use visual cues to systematically review your purpose statement daily.

This is just one example of things you can do to develop your purpose in a strategic way. Choose a way that helps you develop your purpose the best. Remember, your purpose will not find itself. You have to do the leg work.

In the Struggle

What breaks your heart? I have heard it said that every great business or organization started with a broken heart. What do I mean? The painful things often propel us to do something. What do you hate seeing? What upsets you? Often times, you will find your purpose in the struggle.

Something often hurts because God had placed a special grace and passion on your heart to do something about it. In II Corinthians 12:7-10, Paul begs God to take away the thorn from his side. The Bible is not clear about the thorn," but many theologians and commenters suggest it was a frustration, problem, circumstance, or struggle. God's response? "My grace is sufficient for you, for My strength is made perfect in weakness." In other words, where your struggle is, God's strength and grace is also.

There are all sorts of struggles and challenges in the world today: corruption, domestic violence, sex trafficking, racism, mental health care, the economy, our education system, religious persecution, moral decline, gun violence, poverty, and so much more. Obviously, we cannot change the world by ourselves. Some may not be fixed until the day Christ returns. Where there is sin, there will always be struggle. But what struggle in the world really breaks your heart? What challenge rings a bell in your head? What struggle makes you passionate to change? What struggle in life is something you really care about? Although we can't change the world alone, there are struggles where God can use you to make a difference and create an impact.

My quest it to help those who are unsure about that they are called to do. I want folks to see and live to their full potential. So, I would like you to help me in my struggle, by finding your own.

Sound good?

Questions:

- What are things other people say you do very well or that come easy to you?
- What really breaks your heart?
- What are the things you care about that others may not care as deeply about?

- In your quiet time with the Lord, is there anything you feel God is leading you to do as your purpose?
- After utilizing one of the resources listed above, do you sense any direction or clarity about your purpose?

SEVEN

Don't Believe Yourself

Have you ever heard yourself talking? Maybe you saw or
heard a recording of yourself? I don't like hearing myself
talk. It can be one of the most uncomfortable moments to
experience. I can't speak for everyone, but most of the
people I have talked to feel the same way. Over the years,
however, I have come to understand the reason we don't like
it is because our own voice is the one we listen to the most.
And if we're not careful, our voice is the one lying to us the
most about our purpose, our identity, and our perspectives.
Perhaps the biggest lies we've believed are the ones we've
told ourselves.

In this chapter, my goal is to help us uncover the lies we
have told ourselves and replace them with the truth. First,
we have to realize how deceitful we can be to ourselves. In
Jeremiah 17:9 it says

The heart is deceitful above all things and beyond cure. Who can understand it?

This verse uses the heart as a metaphor and paints a picture of how emotions and human will can lead us down a destructive path and cause us to make decisions based off of lies we have told ourselves. But this passage from the Old Testament is not intended to describe the heart of a New Testament believer, someone who has accepted Jesus and understand how God promises to write His law on our hearts and speak to them. At the same time, I want to use this scripture to show how we exhibit the tendency to believe deceitful lies from our hearts, our own will, and our emotions.

One day I was visiting a friend's house in Orlando, FL. After I left, I got on the highway. Within ten minutes I realized I had left my backpack. I grabbed my GPS and changed the directions to lead me back. My GPS told me where to go and the time it would take: *45 minutes.* I couldn't believe it. I double checked, tripled checked. The calculation was correct. Due to traffic, my GPS re-routed me on a longer route. I was flustered, angry, and impatient. Part of me said, "I don't need the backpack that bad, maybe I should just leave it there." But I went to go get it anyway. I went where I was told and waited in traffic. The moment my friend opened the door, I said, "This is why I would never move to Orlando."

Almost instantaneously, I regretted it. I wanted to grab the words and put them back in my mouth. I knew I had said something potentially damaging to my future. I let my emotions get the better of me.

Later, I told other people what happened and what I said. A year later, my pastor called and asked me to move to Orlando to help with building a new church. I saw the moment on my friend's porch in instant replay. "This is why I would never move to Orlando."

I chuckled as I realized I had two choices: Believe the lie I told myself or walk in faith. Happily, I rejected the lie and moved to Orlando to assist with the church.

Your words were certainly different. Maybe they were, "I would never have time to do that," or "There is no one out there for me," or "I could never accomplish that,, or "I am not capable." If you have ever made a similar statement, you probably lied to yourself.

Our emotions, experiences, and feelings will cause us to say things to ourselves that limit our capabilities. All it takes is one small lie to inhibit ourselves. However, when examining it further, you're not just inhibiting yourself, you're inhibiting God's ability to move through you. When you tell yourself that you can't do something, or you would never be able to achieve something, in reality you are limiting the power of God to do those things through you because of your lack of belief.

I understand this book is about positivity and finding the

upbeat perspective. Allow me to be more positive. I am positive you are limiting the power of God when you tell yourself you will never do something! God can do exceedingly, abundantly more than we think, ask, or imagine according to the power of God at work in us (Ephesians 3:20). The things God wants to do through our lives are beyond what we think we can do. If something seems too impossible in your own strength, it is probably from God and it will compel you to call on Him and believe in Him to achieve it.

If you find yourself telling the lie of, "I will never achieve this; I won't amount to much; I can't do it," or something similar, here are a few things you can do to combat the lies.

First, getting rid of negative self-talk. If you think about it, we never intentionally ask for negative self-talk, it just comes. We never have to pause and say something negative about ourselves, our situations, or fears. No, negative self-talk is almost automatically hardwired to kick in whenever we face challenging situations. An article published by the National Science Foundation noted that 80 – 90% of our thoughts are negative. Additionally, 95% of our thoughts are repetitive. Think about it. Do the math. We have constant, on-going negative thoughts constantly being repeated in our minds. If we let them stay, we are allowing them to overtake and consume our brains with negativity. It's like watching mold grow and doing nothing about it. Instead, we must get rid of them. In II Corinthians 10:5 (NIV), it reads: "We demolish arguments and every pretension that sets itself up against the knowledge of God, and we take captive every thought to make it obedient to Christ."

We have the responsibility of taking casting down negative thoughts – removing them. Here are a few practical ways.

- Writing them out: Have you ever written down what is going on in your head? Have you ever taken the time to write out the negative thoughts you have about yourself, others, or a situation? I have, and if you ever saw my journal and some of my thoughts, you would think I am weird. However, whenever you write these thoughts down, you are diminishing their power by getting them out of your head and onto paper (or your device). By simply transitioning these thoughts to words, you're beginning to see how atrocious some of your thoughts are, which helps keep them out of your head. After writing them down, read them and ask yourself, "Is that true? Is that really the way God thinks about me or about this situation?"

- Articulating your thoughts: If you're not able to write them down, you can out loud. This has a very similar effect to writing them down. Speaking them out loud helps you realize how awful some of those thoughts are. Can you imagine having the thought, "I am not good enough," then questioning it out loud by answering "Am I not good enough"? Asking it out loud allows you (and more

importantly God) to intervene against those
negative thoughts even as you realize how negative
they are.

- Telling God about your thoughts: Prayer is simply a
conversation. You talk to God and God talks back
to you. Have a conversation with God about your
negative thoughts. You can speak aloud or journal
about your thoughts. David wrote many of the
psalms. Some are simply David's prayers to God –
the Shepherd King expressing how he feels and the
thoughts he has. People might not be able to handle
your thoughts, but God always can!

- Telling others: It is important to surround ourselves
with people who love us enough to tell us the truth.
It is our responsibility to seek out and surround
ourselves with people who we can trust. This can
be a pastor, small group leader, board member,
boss, therapist, counselor, parent, coach, etc. Once
we have these people in our lives, telling them some
of the thoughts we have is a sure way to help
diminish negativity's power. Invite your friends to
challenge your thoughts. You can pose your
thought as a question. For example: "Hey I have
been thinking I'm not cut out for this. I could be
wrong, what do you think?"

After you have cast negative thoughts down, the more
important step is inviting in the positive thoughts. The
uplifting thoughts. The thoughts that are obedient to Christ.

This is the fun part! Filling yourself with positivity is like getting fuel for a fast car. You can go as far and as fast as you can fuel yourself. Many of us have been limiting ourselves as to how far God wants to take us simply because we do not have enough positive thoughts fueling our minds.

By sharing some ways to invite positive thoughts, I hope it will help you walk in the purposes God has for you. Consider a few ways to invite positive thoughts:

- God's word: There is absolutely nothing more positive than the love that God shares to us through His word. I've heard it said that the Bible is a compilation of 66 love letters (the number of books in the Bible) from God to us. If we can approach God's word as a way to fill ourselves with positivity, we can overflow with positive thoughts in our everyday lives. Maybe you're new to reading God's word. There are plenty of resources you can use to learn how to study the Bible. In my early days of my relationship with Christ, I read a book by Robert West called *How to Study The Bible*. He really helps people understand how to approach reading, studying, and retaining the Bible, not just as knowledge but as food for your soul.
- Positive Self Talk: Yes, talking to yourself. One of my favorite authors, Jon Gordan who I mentioned before, once said we should, "learn to talk to ourselves, not listen to ourselves." Again, our thoughts are almost automatic and we don't

always stop them. Instead, we listen to them. If we really want to start believing the truth, we've got to start speaking the truth to ourselves. Have a quiet conversation with yourself. When I was really trying had to lose weight, I looked in the mirror and said, "I don't like what I see." My wife said, "Stop saying what you don't like and start speaking what you want to see." So I started looking in the mirror and saying, "I am the sexist man in the world. It should be a crime to be this fine." (Okay, it was a little over the top, but I lost the weight.)

- Positive Dreaming: When was the last time you sat down with a pen and paper (or notes app on your phone) and asked yourself, "What could my life look like in five years, 10 years, 20 years, or 50 years?" When you dream, you give space for the Holy Spirit to speak to you, show you things, and to develop a motivation for a positive future. It puts all of your day-to-day problems in focus. It reminds you that your current challenges will not always be there, thus removing the positivity killers and inviting positivity builders.

- Positive Music: Music has such a profound effect on our minds, emotions, thoughts, and actions. That is why most people have a workout playlist with intense music to help them perform at a high level. Think about the music you like. Is it music that validates your negative thoughts or does it push you toward more positive thoughts about yourself, others, and your future?

- Meditation: As a Jesus follower and New Testament believer meditation can seem foreign. I believe there are two functions in meditation: one is to empty ourselves, the other is to fill ourselves. I believe meditating to fill ourselves is very powerful. This is the intentional practice of thinking on the things that are true, honorable, pure, lovely, and commendable (Philippians 4:8). This may look like sitting in a quiet place for 30 − 90 seconds breathing and thinking about positive things. It could also involve thinking about Scripture.

Questions:

- What negative thoughts consistently infiltrate your thinking?
- When negative thoughts come, what can you do to cast them down?
- What ways can you remove and replace your negative thoughts with positive ones?

EIGHT

My Past Defines Me

Once upon a time, there was an baby elephant tied to a tree. Twenty feet of rope secured him by the neck. The elephant was comfortable and well taken care of. The elephant was a circus elephant. He was secured every day after the show. Circling this tree day after day, the elephant created a deep trough in the ground 20 feet in diameter. Years passed and the elephant grew accustomed to walking his little circuit. Years went by and eventually it was time for this elephant to retire. The elephant was released, but after the rope was removed and he was "free," the elephant would never move more than 20 feet away from the tree.

This story reminds us a how we are. Words, decisions, challenges, shortcomings, and trauma have created a pathway of thinking and living that prevents us from moving forward into our future. Like the elephant, we choose to stay in the deep trough we have created instead of trusting God to rewrite our story and show us a new path, and new way!

When I was eight or nine years old, I was playing tee-ball. I had always been a jovial person. I found joy in the little things. When I walked up to the plate, I was always smiling from ear to ear. One day, the coach said, "Be serious, stay focused, pay attention to the ball, and stop smiling so much!" *I get the focus on the ball part, but what does smiling have to do with it,* my little brain thought. I loved to smile. I thought smiling was good. I was happy and smiling was an expression of my happiness. So, I correlated being focused with being unhappy. To this day, I can recall the (bad) advice. It's like it happened yesterday. It left a lasting impression.

Fortunately, I did not let the coach's bad advice crush my spirit – thank God! What about you? Have you let something in your past strangle your future?

Unfortunately, many of us fall into the lie, "My past defines me." It doesn't help that we live in a cancel culture. While the exact definition of "cancel culture" is still evolving, it often involves a person or group of people who are seeking to discredit and withdraw support based off an action someone has taken recently or in the past. With this pressure, many of us are afraid to move forward or to do things that might bring attention. We don't want to be discredited. Remember this – it doesn't matter what someone says about you or who withdraws support. If God is for you, who can be against you?

What, then, shall we say in response to these things? If God is for us, who can be against us? (Romans 8:31)

When we have a mindset focused on God's support, He will use you in a mighty way!

I get what you may be thinking: "Easier said than done." So I want to help you. I want to provide you with some practical ideas designed to keep you from allowing your past to detour you and redefining your future!

What will matter most in 10 or 100 years?

- This question makes you think. It should make you realign your focus and priorities of what really matters most to you. Many times the small things in our past try to convince us they are going to make a big impact in our future. Not true. Think about it. Will what someone thought about you or said about the mistake you made really matter in 10 years? What about 100 years. Chances are it won't. If you are struggling with the lie that your past has defined you, ask if what you have done in your past will really make much of a difference in 100 years. I believe you will be more encouraged with what you do in the next 10 years than by what has happened to you in the past five.

Learn From the Past

What has been will be again, what has been done will be
done again; there is nothing new under the sun. Ecclesiastes
1:9 (NIV)

- King Solomon, referred to in the Bible as "the
  wisest man," wrote Ecclesiastes. When he writes
  "there is nothing new under the sun," we might
  wonder what he means. Whenever I was in college,
  one of my jobs was working at a Bingo Hall. I had
  the responsibility to call bingo numbers and
  confirm winners. Other than the big tips and easy
  work load, what I enjoyed the most was being
  around men and women who were older than me.
  The average age of the individuals who came to
  this Bingo Hall was around 65.These men and
  woman treated me like a son or grandson. They
  would bring me food, invite me to dinners, bring
  gifts, and – what I enjoyed the most – share with
  me wisdom and insight about the future based off
  of what they had experienced in their past. I loved
  to hear their stories of their marriages, their
  families, their careers, their outlook on politics, and
  the various challenges they have lived through and
  learned from. I learned so much from them and a
  lot of the wisdom and understanding I have today
  can be attributed to these older men and women.
  They had so much life experience, but the wisdom

they possessed was nowhere close to what King Solomon had. So when I hear "there is nothing new under the sun," I believe it. We can learn a lot from the past. And the past can teach us about the future. Whether it is our past or someone else's, we can look back and learn from it! Ask questions like, "How can I avoid that same problem?" "Based off of their experiences, what can I apply to my life?" "What would my life look like if I avoided the same issue?" "Who in my life has lived through the challenge I am facing?"

Fail Forward

• Without a doubt we all make mistakes, but mistakes do not mark us as failures. What separates failures from success can be found in a person's ability to move forward after falling down. The definition of insanity if often said to be "doing the same thing over and over and expecting different results."[1] Assess the results you get. If you do not like them, learn how to do things differently. My pastor says it this way, "If you don't like the harvest that is growing, change the seed that you're sowing!" A failure or mistake is not the time to beat yourself up or quit. Instead, it is an opportunity to consider the results, figure out what's working well and what isn't, then try it again another way.

Turn your Mess into a Message

- Some of us may look at the life we've been given as a disadvantage or the things we've encountered as setbacks. That's a limited perspective. When viewed the right way, everything thing in your past can be a testimony designed to help yourself and others in the future. In other words, you can take your mess and turn it into a message of hope for others to hear. You may not have had parents or perhaps yours weren't the greatest. Your reality simply means you have a message on what not to do. You can encourage yourself and others to strive to be better examples as parents. What if someone you loved died of heart disease? You have a message of the importance of healthy eating. Perhaps you start an gym or an organization in the honor of your loved one and teach people a better way to live. My father's situation was a mess, but I continue to use it as a message of hope for others. The Lord has used my tale of losing my dad at 15 to give hope to and help people heal from wounds they suffered in childhood. In addition, I have a greater appreciation for being a father. I know how important my presence is in my children's lives.

Questions:

- What negative past experiences have tried to affect your present or future progress?
- How can you take the messes of your life and use them to encourage others?
- What challenges have you experienced that you can allow God to use to encourage others?

NINE

Get Started

If you're anything like me, you don't like long lines. Whether its traffic, the grocery store, or airport security, I avoid long lines like they are a plague. Over the years I have calmed down a bit and learned to soak up the moments while I'm waiting. I try to find something positive in a long line. But a while back, I wasn't so patient. I was at a Church conference (of all places to be impatient) and I was ready to get something to eat. I saw the long line of people who were walking towards the exit and I thought, *No way, I am going to starve if I stand in this line, there has to be a faster way!* I was leading the way for a group of people. I saw a door. It looked like it was "restricted access" door, but I turned around to the people who were behind me and said, "I think I am going to go through there." They looked at me like I was crazy, but when they saw the tenacity in my eyes (I was really hungry), they followed.

Some of them were telling me, "We shouldn't," and "We're not sure where that door leads," and "What if we get in trouble?" But I made up my mind. I would rather get in trouble than stand in a line.

The door led to a stairwell. We walked down and straight to the parking lot. We got in and drove to get something to eat. Praise God!

As I look back on the story, it reminds me of how many times we set out to do something but stop when we're faced with fear, excuses, or some obstacle. We have all sorts of "doors" standing in the way of our dreams, plans, and purposes. But those doors can't stop us. Go ahead – take a step!

No matter where you are in life, whether your fresh out of high school waiting to take a leap of faith or you're retired and trying to figure out what do with the remaining time on Earth, we all can take a step. Small our big, there is a step to take. What is yours? Is it writing a business plan? Is it meeting with a certain person? Is it constructing an outline? What small step can you take today that will make an impact tomorrow?

Wherever you are and whatever you're doing, you can take a step. No matter how small it is, take it. Whatever you do – just don't stay stagnant. Don't stay still – move!

Maybe you're saying, "But I don't have any motivation to move." Maybe you have the plans, you have the goals, but you lack the motivation to accomplish these things. Or perhaps you seem so far off course from your original plans that the pain of re-routing feels paralyzing.

There is no greater motivation than the fear of the Lord. There is a healthy fear of God. A deep reverence of Him. In his book, *The Awe of God*, John Birvere describes the difference between being afraid of God and having a healthy and holy fear of God. A healthy fear of God is where you do not want to disappoint, grieve, or step out of line with what God wants you to do. It's a knowing you will have to give an account of your actions before God and you are motivated to obey God out of the love you have for Him. A holy fear of God aims to hear the words, "Well done," at the end of your life. I am in fear of getting to the end of my life and hearing "Son, why didn't you do what I asked you to?" We all will have to stand before God and give an account for our actions and I am not okay with telling God I didn't do what He wanted me to do because I was too busy, too afraid, or too worried about what people would think. Listen to Paul's reminder in Romans 14:

> It is written: "As surely as I live, says the Lord, every knee will bow before Me; every tongue will confess to God." So then, each of us will give an account of himself to God.

The fear of God keeps me motivated to obey Him, to be faithful to Him, and to follow His leading because I know I will have to give an account to Him. Unfortunately, too many of us live without the fear of God and we're failing to complete our God-given assignments on this side of heaven.

The late Dr. Myles Monroe made one of the most profound statements I have ever heard. He said, "The most valuable place in the world is the cemetery." Like many, I paused for a moment and wondered why and how. He went on to explain. He said in the cemetery there are many dead dreams, unwritten books, paintings to be painted, business that never started, unrealized ideas, and unfulfilled calls and purposes because people died without giving birth to the things God placed on the inside of them.

My hope is for you to give birth to everything that God put on the inside of you. To obey Him when it hurts, to obey Him with it's not convenient, to obey Him to completion.

The biggest lie we have to unlearn is "I need more _____." You fill in the blank. Maybe it's time, money, education, sleep, energy, vision, people, space, or something else. Yes, we could all use a little more of everything to make our plans more effective, but our insufficiency shouldn't be an excuse to keep us from starting. Many of us, including myself, have made a statement like the one above. And when I thought it was true, it kept me paralyzed in unproductivity. I couldn't take a step because what I wanted to accomplish seemed out of reach. Let me assure you, what God wants you to do will be out of reach. He will show us a vision of our future that will seem impossible. I've heard it said, "God won't give you a life where He isn't necessary". Many times He makes it seem impossible so we will rely on Him! If your dreams, visions and plans seem attainable in your own strength, they may not be from God.

So here's the antidote to the disease of fear: Take a step. No matter how far, how large, or how scary the plans God has for you are, take a step. Maybe your step will lead you to find the plans He has for you. Either way, we need to take it. I love what my pastor says, "God will give you more on your way than before you begin." As you start taking steps in the unknown, God will begin to give you a clearer picture of what to do, where to go, and to whom to speak.

One of my favorite scriptures is Psalm 119:105. It says, "Your word is a lamp to my feet and a light to my path." I love the imagery. A lamp isn't a spotlight, it's not a household kitchen light and it's not a massive search and rescue light. A lamp doesn't give off a lot of light. A lamp will typically only show you what is right in front of you. If I were in the pitch-black woods, the last thing I would want is a lamp. This is the God we serve. He gives us just enough direction to show us the path right in front of us. He does not reveal the whole forest, the whole plan, or the whole route. Sometimes all He will give us is one step to take – one at a time.

What is your step? What do you need to begin? What is God leading you to do next? Maybe you don't know. When I am trying to figure out my first step or my next step, here are some practical things I do.

1. **Make some quiet time.** Notice I said, "Make it," not, "Find it." We live in a very distracting world, full of things fighting for our time and

attention. When I find myself struggling to hear
from God, I have to cut out, turn off, and get away
from the distracting things. At the time of this
writing, the biggest distraction was my kids. I can't
cut them out! So I had to make quiet time. Many
times I went to bed early (sometimes as early as
7:30 pm when the sun was still up) and wake up a
few hours before my kids just to spend time writing.
In your case, maybe instead of catching up on the
new episode of your favorite show, read a chapter
of the Bible. Instead of reaching for your phone to
scroll on Instagram, put your phone aside and take
a 10 minute walk with no devices and talk to God. I
like to sit outside watching the sun come up with
worship music in the background and my notes
open, waiting and expecting God to speak. There
are plenty of ways we can make quite time in our
lives. If we want God to speak to us and we want to
hear Him, we should make time for Him.

2. **Get my will out of the way.** The biggest enemy
   to God's will is our will. When trying to hear from
   God and figuring out what our first or next step is,
   we need to get our will out of the way. This often is
   the major reason we don't hear from Him. We're
   too fixated on what we want, so we can't hear what
   He wants. If we really want to know His will for
   our lives, we need to get our will completely out of
   the way. In Romans 12: 1-2 it says, "And so, dear
   brothers and sisters, I plead with you to give your

bodies to God because of all he has done for you. Let them be a living and holy sacrifice—the kind he will find acceptable. This is truly the way to worship him. Don't copy the behavior and customs of this world, but let God transform you into a new person by changing the way you think. Then you will learn to know God's will for you, which is good and pleasing and perfect." I have heard the second part of this passage many times, but what comes right before it is just as important. *Be a living and holy sacrifice.* Our lives should be sacrifices to God, something we lay down and allow to die before Him. Am I saying you have to die for God? No, not necessarily, but our selfish dreams and desires have to die so the dreams and desires God has for us can come alive in us.

3. **Listen to the voice of the Holy Spirit.** When I first heard about listening to God's voice or hearing from God, I was very intimidated. I didn't grow up hearing a lot about God speaking to people or hearing people say, "God told me..." The few times I did hear about it growing up, it was often depicted in movies as weird or talked about by friends as strange. It wasn't until I investigated for myself and started growing in my relationship with Jesus that I learned hearing from God is both attainable and available. Hearing from God may be different for everyone. When I first started growing in my relationship with God, I felt like God spoke

to me mostly through writing. I would take a pen and paper, write my questions or prayers out then I would pause and ask myself, "What would God say about this?" From there I began to develop my faith to believe God can speak to me. I started going from journaling to hearing God as an inner voice. It wasn't audible (although I have heard some people do hear audibly). It was more of a quiet inner voice. It flowed from my spirit through my mind but it was different from a thought. It sounded a little like my voice and a little like my pastor's voice, but it was distinct enough to be something else. I knew it wasn't my voice because when I heard it, it created a reaction in my soul. I felt refreshed, renewed, rejuvenated, relaxed, and overjoyed. It was like water to a dehydrated man. If you have never heard God speak to you, I want to encourage you, He is eager to speak to you. Have faith and listen!

4. **Read God's word.** The voice of the Holy Spirit and God's word will never contradict. As I read more of God's word I started hearing God even more. Words jumped off of the pages of the Bible straight to my heart, bringing life to dry bones. God's word is alive, active, and has the power to discern the thoughts and intentions of our hearts (Hebrews 4:12). When we read God's word, it will speak to our heart, judge our motives, and provide clarity around seemingly confusing decisions.

Whether it is a story of an Old Testament man or woman of God, hearing about the mistakes of the Apostles, or reading about the life of Jesus, God's word is more than a book with information. It brings our bodies, souls, and spirits inspiration. When you are searching for a first step or next step, believe God can use His word to speak directly to you.

5. **Confide in trusted companions.** God can speak to us directly, through His word and also through people. If you don't have them already, I would encourage you to have three to five people who you trust and allow to speak into your life – people you know who have permission to speak into your future and correct you when you're wrong. The Bible says in Proverbs 11:4, "Where there is no counsel, the people fall; But in the multitude of counselors there is safety." Before taking a step, confide in the people who will help you with direction. This could be a parent, a pastor, a mentor, or someone else you deem as wise and godly – someone who has your best intentions at heart.

Questions:

- What awaits on the other side of our pain, sorrow, excuses or fear?

- What would your life look like if you pushed past your pre-conceived limits?
- What next step do you need to take?
- Who are people you can trust to help hold you accountable to taking you next steps?

Author's Note

I hope and pray this book has inspired you to take a step towards a future filled with God's promises. There is no better feeling than one of fulfilment – knowing and doing something bigger than you. God has something special planned in your future. It is bigger than you can ever think ask or imagine. He is waiting for you to stop believing the lies and to take a step towards His truth. Together, let's live a positive life and make a profound difference in the world. It all starts with a positive perspective!

Notes

1. The Lies We Believe

1. Stephen Hawking to the Hong Kong University of Science and Technology in 2006.
2. https://www.smithsonianmag.com/history/why-martin-luther-king-had-75-percent-disapproval-rating-year-he-died-180968664/

3. God Made This Happen

1. https://www.cdc.gov/nchs/pressroom/pod-casts/2022/20220107/20220107.htm
2. https://www.cdc.gov/mmwr/volumes/69/wr/mm6924e2.htm
3. https://en.wikipedia.org/wiki/2020_California_wild-fires#:~:text=Lightning%20sparked%20a%20slow%2Dgrow-ing%20fire%20in%20inaccessible%20terrain.&text=Multi%2D-fire%20incident%20that%20includes,%3B%205%20in-juries%3B%206%20fatalities.
4. https://en.wikipedia.org/wiki/Chadwick_Boseman
5. https://en.wikipedia.org/wiki/Kobe_Bryant
6. Originally: "If you don't stand for something…" Attributed to Alexander Hamilton and others.

5. If That Hadn't Happened, I Would Be Farther Along By Now

1. Malcolm Gladwell, *David and Goliath*

8. My Past Defines Me

1. Often attributed, without foundation, to Albert Einstein.

Printed in the USA
CPSIA information can be obtained
at www.ICGtesting.com
LVHW051112060524
779124LV00011B/898